What's the Issue?

WHAT ARE STUDENT RIGHTS?

By A

KidHaven PUBLISHING

Published in 2020 by
KidHaven Publishing, an Imprint of Greenhaven Publishing, LLC
353 3rd Avenue
Suite 255
New York, NY 10010

Designer: Deanna Paternostro
Editor: Katie Kawa

Photo credits: Cover (top), p. 13 (bottom) Monkey Business Images/Shutterstock.com; cover (bottom) LightField Studios/Shutterstock.com; pp. 5 (top), 7 (inset), 13 (top) Bettmann/Contributor/Bettmann/Getty Images; p. 5 (bottom) Ronen Tivony/NurPhoto via Getty Images; p. 7 (main) ass29/Shutterstock.com; p. 9 bakdc/Shutterstock.com; p. 11 (top) Rido/Shutterstock.com; p. 11 (bottom) Brocreative/Shutterstock.com; p. 14 Rawpixel.com/Shutterstock.com; p. 15 wavebreakmedia/Shutterstock.com; p. 16 Paul Howell/Liaison/Getty Images; p. 17 Oksana Kuzmina/Shutterstock.com; p. 19 SpeedKingz/Shutterstock.com; p. 21 best_vector/Shutterstock.com.

Cataloging-in-Publication Data

Names: Rogers, Amy B.
Title: What are student rights? / Amy B. Rogers.
Description: New York : KidHaven Publishing, 2020. | Series: What's the issue? | Includes glossary and index.
Identifiers: ISBN 9781534532359 (pbk.) | ISBN 9781534532199 (library bound) | ISBN 9781534532397 (6 pack) | ISBN 9781534532281 (ebook)
Subjects: LCSH: Students–Legal status, laws, etc.–United States–Juvenile literature. | Students–Civil rights–United States–Juvenile literature. | Educational law and legislation–United States–Juvenile literature. | Student movements–Juvenile literature.
Classification: LCC KF4150.R64 2020 | DDC 344.73'0793–dc23

Printed in the United States of America

Some of the images in this book illustrate individuals who are models. The depictions do not imply actual situations or events.

CPSIA compliance information: Batch #BW20KL: For further information contact Greenhaven Publishing LLC, New York, New York at 1-844-317-7404.

Please visit our website, www.greenhavenpublishing.com. For a free color catalog of all our high-quality books, call toll free 1-844-317-7404 or fax 1-844-317-7405.

CONTENTS

Know Your Rights!

Most people know that adults in the United States have rights that can't be taken away. These include the right to free speech and the right to be **protected** against unlawful searches.

Do kids have these same rights? This isn't always an easy question to answer. The rights of children and young adults in school—also known as student rights—have changed over time and are continuing to change to deal with modern problems, such as **cyberbullying**. It's important to know your rights in school, so keep reading to learn more about this issue!

Facing the Facts

Some students go to public schools, which are run with money from the government. Others go to private schools, which are run with money from private individuals and groups, such as churches. Students in private schools only have rights that are granted by that school. In general, this book deals with student rights in public schools.

Students have rights, and they've used those rights throughout history to stand up for themselves and for what they believe. The fight for student rights hasn't always been easy, and it's a fight that continues today!

5

Making the Case for Student Rights

Many of the most well-known rights Americans have are part of the First **Amendment** to the U.S. Constitution, which is the document that set up how the country is run. It's the job of the U.S. Supreme Court to decide how this amendment applies to different **situations**.

In 1969, the Supreme Court made an important ruling about student rights in the case of *Tinker v. Des Moines Independent Community School District*. The court said that students don't lose their First Amendment rights at school unless they're doing something that keeps the school from running properly.

Facing the Facts

Tinker v. Des Moines Independent Community School District dealt with high school students who wanted to wear black armbands to show that they were against the **Vietnam War**. The Supreme Court ruled that the students had the right to wear the armbands.

First Amendment Freedoms

freedom of speech

the freedom to
speak or act—or
not to speak or act

freedom of the press

the freedom to
write, report on
television or the
radio, or post
online about
the truth

freedom of religion

the freedom to
have whatever
belief system
one chooses

freedom to peaceably
assemble

the freedom to
peacefully gather
in groups

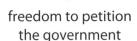

freedom to petition
the government

the freedom to ask
the government
to fix things that
are wrong

The First Amendment grants Americans the right to exercise all
of these freedoms without being **punished** by the government.
It's up to the Supreme Court to decide how these freedoms can
be exercised in today's world—including in today's classrooms.

7

Walking Out

In 2018, thousands of students across the United States walked out of their classes to take a stand against gun **violence**. This raised the question of whether or not students had the right to walk out of school.

Students can be punished for missing school because of a walkout. However, they can't be punished more strongly because of what they're **protesting**. They also can't be punished for taking part in a protest that doesn't get in the way of school activities, such as a protest that takes place in another location after school or on a weekend.

Facing the Facts

In 1988, the Supreme Court ruled that school officials could control what was printed in a school's newspaper if they had educational concerns about it. People who fight for student rights believe this ruling went against the idea of a free student press.

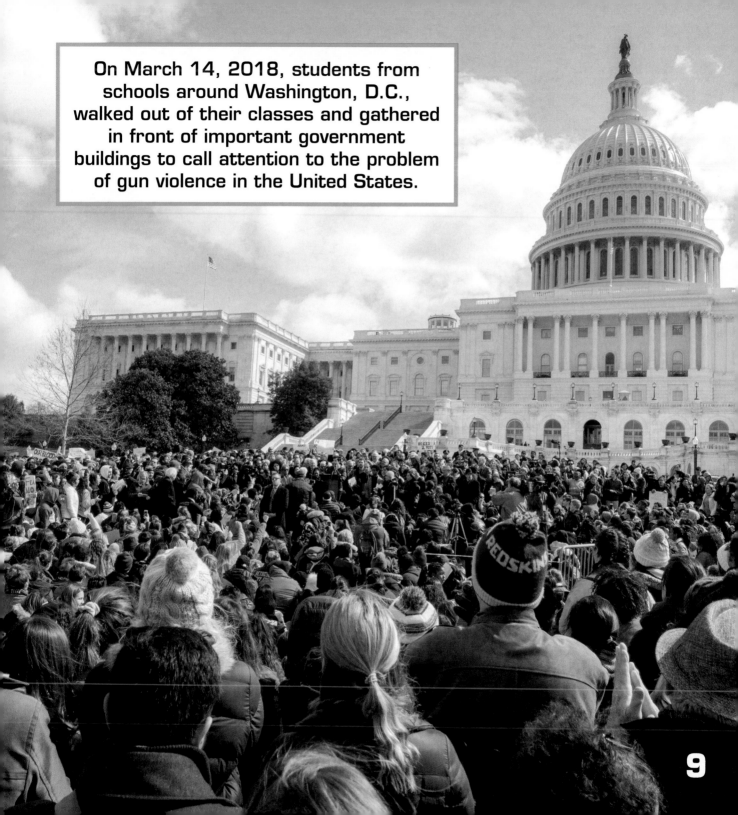

On March 14, 2018, students from schools around Washington, D.C., walked out of their classes and gathered in front of important government buildings to call attention to the problem of gun violence in the United States.

9

Watching What You Wear

The First Amendment protects what's often called freedom of expression, or the way a person shows what they're thinking or feeling. Clothing is one form of expression, and the right to express yourself through your clothing is an important part of growing up.

Schools often have dress codes that state what students can and can't wear. However, these dress codes can't be used to punish certain groups, such as girls or African Americans. Schools can only ban clothing that gets in the way of learning. Otherwise, students have the right to freely choose what to wear.

Facing the Facts

Students can freely express their religion in school, as long as it doesn't get in the way of their learning or other students' school activities. This means they have the right to wear clothing that's important to their religion, such as a head covering.

Most schools have dress codes, but not all of them are fair to all groups of students. If you think your school's dress code unfairly singles out certain students, talk to a trusted adult.

Equal Rights

One of the most important student rights is the right to be protected against discrimination, which happens when one person or group is treated differently than another person or group in a way that's unfair. In 1972, a law was passed to protect students from discrimination based on their sex. This law is known as Title IX, or Title Nine.

Under Title IX, schools that get money from the government must give boys and girls equal opportunities. In addition, all students have the right to feel safe at school and to not be treated differently because of their sex.

Facing the Facts

In the past, many schools discriminated against students because of their race. African Americans were forced to go to separate schools that were often in poor condition. This practice was known as school segregation. In 1954, the Supreme Court ruled that school segregation went against the Constitution, and it was stopped.

Title IX includes school sports. This means girls and boys must have equal opportunities to play sports at school. Because of Title IX, many more girls started playing school sports!

Students with Disabilities

Students with disabilities also have the right to be protected against discrimination. They must be given **access** to services that allow them to have the same quality of education as students without disabilities. These services can include special classrooms, people to help them, and health care.

Students with disabilities also have the right to take part in school activities, such as field trips and clubs. Important laws have been passed to protect these rights and to make sure that all students have the same chance to succeed in school.

STOP BULLYING

Facing the Facts

If a student is being bullied because of their race, background, sex, religion, or disability, their school must actively work to stop the bullying.

Everyone can do their part to respect the rights of students with disabilities and to help them feel included in school activities.

Smartphone Searches

As times have changed, lawmakers, school officials, and the Supreme Court have been asked to think about new student rights issues. Recently, the use of smartphones has led to new questions about a student's right to privacy.

The Fourth Amendment to the U.S. Constitution protects people from unlawful searches. A student's backpack or purse can't be searched without a good reason, and the same is now true for their smartphone. For example, a teacher can't read what's on a student's phone just because they caught them using it in class.

16

Facing the Facts

School officials can search any piece of school property without a student saying it's okay. Lockers and desks are often considered school property.

A teacher can take away a student's phone to punish them for breaking school rules about cell phone use. However, that teacher can't look at what's on the phone. If a teacher asks a student to let them see what's on their phone without a good reason, the student can say no.

Student Rights Outside of School

What are your rights when it comes to the use of your phone outside of school? In most cases, what a student shares on their own phone, computer, or other **device** after school hours can't get them in trouble at school. However, if they use their own device to bully or **threaten** another student outside of school, they can be punished.

Online activity on school computers or other devices is often monitored, or closely watched, by school officials. Because these devices are school property, students don't have the same right to privacy on them as they do on their own devices.

Facing the Facts

Between 2007 and 2016, the percentage of kids who'd been cyberbullied at some point in their life almost doubled.

School officials and lawmakers are working to find a balance between protecting students' right to safety and their right to privacy. For example, if one student is threatening another on **social media** outside of school, many people believe the threatened student's right to safety is more important than the bully's right to privacy.

Rights and Responsibilities

All rights come with **responsibilities**. Students have a responsibility to treat their teachers and classmates with respect. They also shouldn't exercise their rights in a way that makes it impossible for others to learn.

Every school has different rules about what rights students have and how they can exercise them. Schools have a responsibility to let students know what those rules are, and students have a responsibility to educate themselves about those rules. If you feel any of your school's rules are unfair, you can talk to a trusted adult about how to protect your rights.

Facing the Facts

One group that works hard to educate students about their rights and to protect the rights of all Americans is the American Civil Liberties Union, or ACLU.

WHAT CAN YOU DO?

Raise money for groups that protect and fight for student rights.

If you're not sure of your school's rules about certain student rights issues, ask a teacher or school official.

If you think your rights aren't being respected at school, talk to a trusted adult.

When exercising your rights at school, remember to do so in a way that still allows other students to learn.

Learn more about your rights and responsibilities as a student.

Respect the rights of other students.

As a student, you have important rights that should be respected. How will you exercise your rights at school?

GLOSSARY

access: The ability to use or have something.

amendment: A change in the words or meaning of a law or document, such as a constitution.

cyberbullying: The act of bullying someone through online or cell phone messages or posts.

device: A tool used for a certain purpose.

protect: To keep safe.

protest: To speak out strongly against something. Also, an event in which people gather to show they do not like something.

punish: To make someone suffer for doing something wrong.

responsibility: A duty that a person should do.

situation: All the facts, conditions, and events that affect someone or something in a certain time and place.

social media: A collection of websites and applications, or apps, that allow users to interact with each other and create online communities.

threaten: To make someone feel as if they will be harmed.

Vietnam War: A war fought between North Vietnam and its allies and South Vietnam and its allies, including the United States, from the 1950s to the 1970s.

violence: The use of force to harm someone.

FOR MORE INFORMATION

WEBSITES

BrainPOP: Student Rights

www.brainpop.com/socialstudies/usgovernment/studentrights/

The videos, facts, quizzes, and activities on this website help kids learn more about student rights.

My School My Rights

www.myschoolmyrights.com/

This website, which was created for students in California, answers many questions about student rights in ways that can also be useful to students in other states.

BOOKS

Bjorklund, Ruth. *The Bill of Rights: Why It Matters to You*. New York, NY: Children's Press, 2019.

Lynch, Seth. *The Bill of Rights*. New York, NY: Gareth Stevens Publishing, 2019.

Machajewski, Sarah. *American Freedoms: A Look at the First Amendment*. New York, NY: PowerKids Press, 2019.

Publisher's note to educators and parents: Our editors have carefully reviewed these websites to ensure that they are suitable for students. Many websites change frequently, however, and we cannot guarantee that a site's future contents will continue to meet our high standards of quality and educational value. Be advised that students should be closely supervised whenever they access the Internet.

INDEX